To Dear Wendy & Geoff.
with love Jacki & Steve 1998.

GW00643059

Steve Parish

CELEBRATING AUSTRALIA

BRISBANE & BEYOND

Steve Parish
PUBLISHING

Previous pages: Across the Brisbane River to Eagle Street Pier and the Riverside Centre.   *Above:* In springtime, the radiant jacarandas enhance the lush subtropical greens of Brisbane's suburbs.

Introduction

Although I could happily live and work in any Australian city, Brisbane has a very special place in my life. It is a city of infinite variety, superbly located on the banks of the Brisbane River, and with a wealth of picturesque areas in which its people can relax and play. There are so many wonderful, and photogenic, places within a short distance of Brisbane's City Hall — South Bank and the adjoining Cultural Centre, the cliffs and foreshore of Kangaroo Point, the Riverside Centre, with its moored paddlewheelers, the splendid City Botanic Gardens, Mt Coot-tha with its breath-taking view of the coastal plain ... the list could go on and on.

For the nature lover, sun-seeker or fun-seeker, the country close to Brisbane offers incomparable riches: the rainforest magic of the Lamington Plateau; the sun-drenched sands, sea and surf of the Gold Coast with its sophisticated nightlife; the wonderful beaches, lakes and mountains of the Sunshine Coast; the majestic sand dunes and fantastic lakes of Fraser Island; whale-watching at Hervey Bay. The choices of country getaways within easy reach of the city are seemingly limitless, governed only by the traveller's interests and needs.

Brisbane is such a cheerful city, and so multicultural and friendly, that it is not easy to remember that it was originally a dumping-ground for the most rebellious of the convicts transported to New South Wales. In the years since transportation ceased, there have been enormous changes. Perhaps once Brisbane became a free colony its inhabitants set themselves to make up for those sad years, and the incredible natural riches of Queensland gave the resources for development and growth. Certainly the achievements of the wildly successful World Expo '88 catapulted the city into the ranks of top tourist destinations. Today, Brisbane and the surrounding countryside offer world-class entertainment, food, accommodation, and service, added to which are their own special blend of subtropical beauty and Queensland hospitality.

Steve Parish

Following pages: Brisbane city centre seen across Kangaroo Point with New Farm in the foreground. Top right is the Story Bridge.

The city of Brisbane

Brisbane, capital of the State of Queensland, stands on the banks of the Brisbane River which winds itself in a lover's embrace around the heart of the city. It it a prosperous multicultural city of more than one million people.

At the city's centre are the towers of government, industry and commerce, bustling department stores and elegant boutiques, restaurants, theatres and galleries. Gracing the opposite bank of the river are the Cultural Centre and the South Bank Parklands.

Brisbane was established in 1825 as a penal colony to house the worst of convicts transported to this country. Today there are few reminders of the city's origins, but the examples of the nineteenth century's building skills and grand architectural styles that do remain are preserved, restored and adapted to modern-day requirements.

Left: Night falls on Brisbane city and the Story Bridge which spans the river between Fortitude Valley and Kangaroo Point. The lights on the bridge were supplied by the city in 1990 to celebrate its fiftieth anniversary.

George Street at dusk.

City lights

Sunset mellows the historic buildings of Brisbane and turns more modern office high-rises into glittering towers. Nightfall brings crowds enjoying a climate where rain seldom lingers, and where most nights of the year favour informal dressing and outdoor pursuits. Sidewalk cafes and fine restaurants abound in this subtropical city; theatres and cinemas feature the latest hits, and night football and race meetings attract enthusiastic crowds. The Casino which now operates in the impressively restored Treasury Building is a prime attraction for those seeking an exciting night in town.

Above: Brisbane's Treasury Casino, ready for a night's exciting action.

Following pages: Night falls on Brisbane.

A view past the clock tower of Brisbane's Central Station, over the Anzac Memorial and Anzac Square to Post Office Square.

10

The Eternal Flame burns in the Anzac Memorial.

Anzac Square

On Ann Street, opposite Central Station, Brisbane's Anzac Memorial commemorates the Queenslanders who served in the First World War. Monuments to the fallen in other wars stand in Anzac Square nearby. Erected in the 1920s, the Anzac Memorial houses an Eternal Flame and features columns of sandstone encircling a floor of mosaic.

Each year on August 25th the Memorial is the venue for solemn ceremonies of remembrance which honour all those Australians who have served their country in time of war.

Anzac Square forms a green refuge amongst the inner city buildings. The effect of this oasis is continued by Post Office Square, on the other side of which stands the nineteenth-century dignity of Brisbane's General Post Office. Beneath the green of the Squares run modern shopping arcades, linking Ann, Adelaide and Queen Streets.

11

Above: The Riverside Expressway skirts Brisbane's central business district.

The river city

The Brisbane is a beautiful and useful watercourse, which has earned for Queensland's capital the title "River City". Landscaping, the provision of walking and bicycle tracks along its shores, and its suitability for all kinds of water sports have made the calm lower courses of the river ideal for relaxation and recreation. A passenger ferry service travels the Brisbane linking several points on its banks and offering commuters quick, convenient and scenic transport.

Early European explorers found the Brisbane Valley a paradise of tropical vegetation, bordered by rich floodplains. They used terms such as beautiful, picturesque, noble and magnificent in writing of the scenery along the river and thought the area eminently suitable for a settlement. Its richness had supported Aboriginal people for many years.

Today, the Brisbane's banks are lined with parklands and with gracious homes standing in luxuriant gardens. Further inland, it flows between fertile farmlands. It has certainly fulfilled the hopes of those early visitors.

Opposite: The Expressway and Captain Cook Bridge reflected in the river.
Following pages: The natural light imparts varying hues to Brisbane city and the river, seen here at dusk and at dawn.

Brisbane's heritage

The old Customs House has been elegantly refurbished.

In the 1970s, efforts to demolish certain of Brisbane's historic buildings led to renewed interest in their restoration. Today, places such as the old Customs House and the Treasury are showplaces, restored and used for a variety of purposes. City Hall was opened in 1930: built of golden Helidon sandstone, it is noted for its imposing Corinthian columns and sculptures.

City Hall reflected in the pool in King George Square.

Mt Coot-tha

Above: On the viewing platform of the Mt Coot-tha Lookout.

The name "Coot-tha" comes from an Aboriginal phrase meaning "place of honey", and the flanks of this mountain eight kilometres from the centre of Brisbane are ornamented with eucalypt forests and rainforest-bordered streams. A scenic drive winding around the mountain brings visitors to charming picnic points and to the Lookout, from which can be seen a breath-taking panorama. On a clear day, the Border Ranges to the south and the Glasshouse Mountains to the north are also visible.

Above: The Summit Restaurant and Kuta Cafe on Mt Coot-tha.

Following pages: A view of Brisbane city from Mt Coot-tha.

The Mt Coot-tha Botanic Gardens

The Tropical Dome at Mt Coot-tha Botanic Gardens is a huge glasshouse.

In 1828, a site for growing fruit and vegetables for the then convict colony was selected on the bank of the Brisbane River. Today, the area houses Brisbane's City Botanic Gardens, a place for relaxation and festivity for the people of Queensland's capital. A second Botanic Gardens has been established on the lower slopes of Mt Coot-tha, seven kilometres from the city centre.

Water lilies are a feature of Mt Coot-tha's Botanic Gardens.

Mt Coot-tha Botanic Gardens cover 52 hectares and make fine use of natural watercourses. They showcase plants from around the world and theme gardens: a Japanese Garden, Rainforest Garden and Fragrant Garden. Other attractions include lakes and lilies, an excellent restaurant and cafe, the Cosmic Skydome and the Sir Thomas Brisbane Planetarium.

Brisbane's magnificent jacarandas

Four views of Brisbane's sumptuous springtime jacaranda display.

Each springtime, flowering jacaranda trees light Brisbane's streets and gardens in splendour, burning brightly against the sunny skies above. The banks of the Brisbane River are embroidered with beauty and many suburban gardens boast a stunning display of blossom.

Jacaranda blossom, New Farm Park.

At the entrance to the City Botanic Gardens.

The ground beneath a flowering jacaranda is almost as splendid as the tree itself, covered in oriental splendour with fallen blossoms. As the flowers fall, tiny green leaves begin to appear on silver-grey twigs and soon the jacaranda tree is again covered with feathery foliage.

Along the Brisbane River in jacaranda time.

Jacaranda blooms colour suburban gardens and parklands, seen here from above the Walter Taylor Bridge over the Brisbane River.

Queensland Cultural Centre

Three splendid venues make up the Queensland Performing Arts Centre, where world-class artists entertain enthusiastic and knowledgeable audiences. Ballet, opera, plays, musical theatre, solo artists and orchestral concerts are all performed at this superb complex.

Also standing on the Brisbane River foreshore are the Queensland Art Gallery, which is noted for its collection of modern Australian works, and the comprehensive State Library.

Completing the cluster of impressive buildings which make up the Queensland Cultural Centre is the much-loved and much-visited Queensland Museum, which has innovative displays placing emphasis upon the natural world and the fascinating history of the State.

Left: Cascades border the forecourt of the Performing Arts Centre, which lies just over the Victoria Bridge from the centre of Brisbane.

Where people meet

An airy walkway joins the Museum to the Performing Arts Centre.

The Performing Arts Centre, Queensland Museum, Art Gallery, State Library and their neighbour the Convention and Exhibition Centre provide places for people with common interests to meet for education and entertainment. They are marvellously designed to suit Brisbane's sub-tropical climate: the Convention and Exhibition Centre, which stages displays, houses trade fairs and hosts conventions, is particularly striking, with its shady shells sheltering high glassed walls.

A view over South Brisbane to the Convention and Exhibition Centre and the Queensland Cultural Centre.

South Bank Parklands

The Entrance Court of South Bank Parklands.

South Bank Parklands occupy the 16-hectare site of the enormously successful World Expo '88, on the shore of the Brisbane River opposite the city centre. This splendid venue offers year-round entertainment, six annual festivals, a weekend Crafts Village and fascinating theme attractions such as Gondwana Rainforest Sanctuary. Visitors can enjoy the superb restaurants, relax at one of the many cafes, barbecue or picnic. At Kodak Beach, they can swim, build sand castles or learn to scuba dive under the protection of a professional lifeguard.

Close neighbours of the Parklands are the Maritime Museum, Queensland Cultural Centre and the Convention and Exhibition Centre.

Above: The Crafts Village attracts crowds on Friday nights, Saturdays and Sundays.

Above: Canal boats tour the southern perimeter of the Parklands.

Following pages: Kodak Beach, South Bank Parklands.

Eagle Street Pier

The Town Reach of the Brisbane River is bordered by the cliffs of Kangaroo Point on one bank and the City Botanic Gardens and Eagle Street on the other. Eagle Street was named after the bronze-backed, white-breasted Brahminy Kites which still patrol the river and nest in the tallest trees in the Gardens.

Between Eagle Street and the river is the Riverside Centre and Eagle Street Pier, mooring point for the famous *Kookaburra Queen I* and *II* paddlewheelers. These gracious craft progress majestically along the river, allowing their passengers unequalled views of the city while they dine or partake of light refreshments.

Left: The Riverside Centre, between Eagle Street and the Brisbane River, with the *Kookaburra Queen* paddlewheelers moored at Eagle Street Pier.

The Riverside Centre

Brisbane's restaurants, bars and bistros are noted for the variety and excellence of their offerings. Besides enjoying exceptional seafood and Australian dishes using the freshest of fine-quality ingredients, diners can choose from a wide range of international cuisines.

Where better to dine than overlooking the glimmering waters of the Brisbane River? The Riverside Centre is one of many places along the waterfront to offer a variety of places to appreciate gastronomic delights and, in typical Brisbane fashion, the ambiance can vary from relaxed and casual to formal silver service.

Right: The Riverside Centre and Eagle Street Pier at night.
Following pages: The *Kookaburra Queens* at their moorings.

The river at dusk

Many of Brisbane's residents keep pleasure craft moored along the various reaches of the river: the area between Gardens Point and Kangaroo Point is particularly popular. The scene shown here, peaceful at dusk, is part of the site of the thriving Riverside Markets, which fills the foreshore with activity every weekend.

Right: A peaceful moment for Eagle Street Pier and the Riverside Centre.

Riverside Markets

Umbrellas shade stalls at the Riverside Markets.

The Sunday markets held at the Riverside Centre attract large crowds to browse and buy. Works of art, clothing, jewellery, pottery, woodcarvings, floor coverings, indoor and outdoor plants, and a host of other desirable goods can be purchased at stalls set up on a site unequalled for convenience of access or scenic charm.

Satisfied bargain-hunters at the Riverside Markets.

Hospitality unlimited

Park Road, Milton, offers hospitality, indoor and outdoor, with international flair.

Brisbane enjoys a climate which is eminently suited to outdoor living, and the city and its suburbs are full of places to dine in the open air, day or night.

The Regatta Hotel, on Coronation Drive, Toowong, is only one of many establishments to offer wide, shady verandahs and cool gardens in which to enjoy refreshments. The popularity of such traditional "watering holes" is today challenged by that of the sidewalk cafes, bistros and brasseries which have sprung up wherever people enjoy getting together for fun and entertainment. Park Road, Milton, with its miniature replica of a well-known Parisian landmark, is one of the most popular of these venues.

The Regatta Hotel, on Coronation Drive, is famous for its hospitality, and for its elegant balcony railings.

Above: The shining windows of Brisbane's tall towers.

Above: Arch and tower, the Riverside Centre.

Designed for living

In the second half of the twentieth century, Brisbane city's stone, brick and tile buildings were dwarfed by a new architecture made possible by the use of steel frames, electric lifts, air-conditioning and the lavish use of glass, treated to provide protection against the sun's rays, for window walls.

The award-winning Riverside Centre, completed in 1987, is justly famous for its suitability for Brisbane's subtropical climate: aluminium sunshading devices are integrated with the polished granite and glass facade and complex electronic controls regulate internal functions. A striking curved gateway structure, visible at the top of the image at left, links two buildings on either side of a plaza which gives access to the river via wide steps.

An efficient road network facilitates travelling around Brisbane's widespread suburbs. This is the intersection of the Western Freeway and Moggill Road.

An aerial view of the Story Bridge which links the city and Fortitude Valley with Kangaroo Point.

Sculptures on the Brisbane River foreshore, with the cliffs of Kangaroo Point behind.

A view across the Brisbane from Lower River Terrace.

Kangaroo Point

Strolling, jogging, cycling, walking the dog or letting the kids run about and shout — the pathways, tracks and open spaces along the banks of the Brisbane River have endless possibilities for action and relaxation. In some places, works of art have been integrated into the landscape.

The colourful cliffs of Kangaroo Point add to the possibilities for adventure and are a popular place to learn the basics of rock-climbing and abseiling.

Above: A rainforest monarch on Mount Glorious.

Above: A quiet moment in the rainforest.

The green behind Brisbane

Close to Brisbane are a number of protected natural areas enclosed in national parks. Particularly impressive is the 26 500-hectare Brisbane Forest Park, which encompasses dry eucalypt forest, open woodland and lush rainforest. Each habitat has an abundance of wildlife, including many colourful species of birds and, in the eucalypt forests, the appealing, leaf-eating Koala.

Mount Glorious, in Brisbane Forest Park, is one of the most popular wild places close to Brisbane. A short drive from Brisbane's north-western suburbs, it offers lookouts from which magnificent views can be enjoyed, tracks through subtropical rainforest, and well-maintained, pretty picnic grounds and sheltered camping areas.

Following pages: Rainforest in Maiala National Park, in Brisbane Forest Park.

The Gold Coast

The most popular holiday destination in Australia, the Gold Coast is a sweeping stretch of beaches more than 40 kilometres long. From the mouth of the Coomera River south to Coolangatta on the New South Wales border, the golden beaches and rolling breakers are an hour's drive from Brisbane.

The Coast has a yearly average temperature of 27°C and enjoys nearly 300 days of sunshine each year. Its beachside towns offer accommodation and entertainment of international standards and visitors take full advantage of these blessings, spending much of their time swimming, surfing, fishing or just lying around. Many people visit theme parks such as Movie World, Dreamworld or Sea World, while others seek excitement at Jupiters Casino at Broadbeach.

Left: Looking south from above the Spit, along Main Beach and Surfers Paradise. At top right is the estuary of the Nerang River, flowing into the Broadwater.

The sapphire blue Pacific Ocean and broad sweeps of sandy beaches are a source of endless enjoyment for sailors, surfers, sunbathers and fisherfolk.

The Broadwater

Above: Looking over Southport Yacht Club to Marina Mirage and Sea World.

Opposite: Main Beach and the Spit, with the Broadwater beyond.

The Broadwater, where the Nerang River flows to the ocean, is an estuary protected by the long stretch of sand known as the Spit, and by South Stradbroke Island. Sailing and powered craft of all categories, from ocean-going yachts and fishing vessels to houseboats, find the Broadwater safe harbour. It also houses one of the Coast's prime attractions, Sea World, a spectacular marine park where dolphins, whales and sea-lions and a variety of dramatic displays and rides entertain enthralled visitors.

Surfers Paradise

A gateway to fun, Cavill Mall, Surfers Paradise.

The "Surfers Paradise" was originally a hotel at Elston, near Southport, which was popular with the many holiday-makers who camped near the beach or stayed in seaside cottages. In 1925, the Jubilee Bridge across the Nerang River was opened making access from Brisbane easier and, in 1933, hotel-owner Jim Cavill re-named Elston "Surfers Paradise". Today, the vibrant and colourful shopping and entertainment precinct of "Surfers" offers restaurants, nightclubs, bars and boutiques to suit all tastes, with a particular emphasis on helping visitors secure their hearts' desires.

Following pages: Scenes from Surfers Paradise.

The Dolphin Arcade, Surfers Paradise.

Hard Rock Cafe and Funtasia, Paradise Centre, Surfers Paradise.

A wander along the beach stimulates the senses for a day spent shopping or just enjoying the Queensland sun.

South-east Queensland's beaches are among the finest in the world.

Pacific Fair Shopping Centre, Broadbeach.

Gold Coast attractions

Conrad Jupiters Casino and Hotel, Broadbeach.

The Gold Coast is visited by 3 500 000 tourists each year, and the resident population is around 340 000, with an annual growth rate of around four percent. The Gold Coast City Council realises the importance of retaining the spaciousness and charm which have proved great attractions, and developments such as popular Pacific Fair Shopping Centre and Conrad Jupiters Casino and Hotel display fastidious landscaping, as well as imaginative and innovative design.

Following pages: Opulent Raptis Plaza at Surfers Paradise (left), where stands a replica of Michelangelo's David carved from a 33 tonne block of Carrara marble; and (right) inside Pacific Fair Shopping Centre at Broadbeach.

The Queensland/New South Wales border runs down the centre of this headland, with Coolangatta on its northern side and Tweed Heads to the south.

The Gold Coast hinterland

West of the Gold Coast stands the Great Dividing Range. Once timber was harvested from its slopes and its valleys were cleared for farming. Today, a series of National Parks protects some of the world's remaining areas of subtropical rainforest. Much of the area was once a giant volcano, and dramatic landforms have been weathered from its fire-formed rocks.

Two scenic areas, Springbrook National Park, noted for its waterfalls and ancient Antarctic Beech trees, and the dramatic and rugged Mt Warning National Park are closest to the Coast. The eucalypt forests of the lovely Numinbah Valley are refuges for the Koala and many other wild creatures.

Left: The beautiful Numinbah Valley.

Springbrook National Park

A rainforest stream in Springbrook National Park.

Subtropical rainforest is a feature of Springbrook National Park, which lies a short drive inland from the Gold Coast. Clear mountain streams tumbling over ledges of rock to form scenic waterfalls are common in this reserve. The shade of the rainforest canopy does not reach the banks of these streams, and they are alive with butterflies, dragonflies and other insects, while the waters harbour freshwater crays and long-legged, goggle-eyes frogs.

Purlingbrook Falls, in Springbrook National Park.

Natural Bridge

The fantastic Natural Bridge in Springbrook National Park is today a cool and peaceful place, where silver water cascades into a shimmering pool. It was born of volcanic fire, aeons ago, when an enormous volcano belched molten lava across the area which is now south-eastern Queensland. The lava cooled, became solid and, over long ages, was fretted by wind and water into picturesque landforms. The arch is formed by hard rock which remained when softer supporting elements were eroded away.

Right: Natural Bridge, Springbrook National Park.

Chalahn Falls, Lamington National Park.

Elabana Falls, Lamington National Park.

Lamington National Park

Lamington National Park and the Border Ranges National Park offer memorable rainforest experiences, from walking beneath Antarctic Beech trees which were young when the Roman Empire declined, to watching the mating dances of the flamboyant bowerbirds and the reclusive Albert's Lyrebird. Walking tracks give access to some of Australia's most stunning views, and to pools and waterfalls such as those shown here, which are magical in their beauty.

Mt Tamborine

Mt Tamborine is a plateau about 8 kilometres long and 5 kilometres wide, situated just south of Brisbane. The area was opened up by loggers in the late 1800s and today some majestic stands of forest and graceful groves of native palms are preserved in the nine small national parks declared on the plateau. Curtis Falls, in Joalah National Park, a noted beauty spot, is named after four brothers who operated a steam-driven timber mill in the district in the 1880s.

The plateau is a favourite place for birdwatchers and other nature lovers, and the area is noted for its cottage industries, with craftspeople and artists marketing their creations through galleries and shops in the hamlets of North Tamborine, Eagle Heights and Mt Tamborine. It is a short drive from Brisbane and the Gold Coast.

Opposite: A walking track in Joalah National Park, on Mt Tamborine.

87

The scenic beauty north of Brisbane

The Glasshouse Mountains, seen from Bribie Island across Pumicestone Passage.

Just north of Brisbane, the commencement of the Sunshine Coast, a holiday area of infinite variety and scenic charm, is signposted by a group of ancient volcanic cores named the Glasshouse Mountains by Captain Cook as he sailed up the coast of Queensland in the barque *Endeavour* in 1770.

The Sunshine Coast stretches from Bribie Island and Caloundra in the south to Double Island Point in the north. This superb stretch of coastline is a famous area for fishing and sailing.

Fishing off the beach at sunrise on the Sunshine Coast.

Mooloolaba is noted for its safe harbour.

An aerial view of Mooloolaba, overlooking the jetties at Underwater World.

Maroochydore overlooks the estuary of the Maroochy River.

Mooloolaba and Maroochydore

The port of Mooloolaba is home to a fleet of fishing and prawning vessels, as well as to countless pleasure craft. It is a holiday resort noted for good fishing, fine food and excellent accommodation. Maroochydore, just to the north of Mooloolaba, lies between two of Australia's finest beaches. The town's name is derived from the Aboriginal term for the Black Swan, and the estuary of the Maroochy River, which is navigable for up to 80 kilometres upstream, is a haunt for waterbirds of all kinds.

Noosa

Sunseekers on Noosa Beach.

Noosa offers sunseekers a splendid lifestyle in a town where it is law that no building shall be higher than the trees. Restaurants, shops and hotels have elegantly accommodated this rule. Within easy access of the town are Noosa National Park and the magnificent waterways of the Noosa River and its accompanying lakes.

Above: A lazy day at Granite Bay, Noosa National Park.

Pages 94-97: Aerial views of Noosa and Noosa National Park.

Sunshine Coast hinterland

The Glasshouse Mountains seen from McCarthys Lookout, on the Great Dividing Range.

Montville, Maleny, Kenilworth and Imbil are typical of the small towns nestled in the folds of the ranges west from the Sunshine Coast. They are noted for their tropical fruits and dairy cattle, and also as centres for artists, who find creative inspiration amongst such natural beauty.

Above: Baroon Pocket Dam, near Montville, in the ranges behind the Sunshine Coast.   *Following pages* At the northern end of the Sunshine Coast, Cooloola Beach has become a 4WD motorway.

The Blackall and Conondale Ranges, parts of the Great Dividing Range, lie inland from the Sunshine Coast. Some scenic areas are protected in national parks, and much is classed as state forest. Where arable mountain land is under cultivation, it may present the park-like aspect shown above.

Lake McKenzie stands in the midst of a forest of blackbutt trees.

102

Fraser Island

A sand dune and Lake Wabby, deepest of Fraser Island's lakes.

The mighty sand deposit which is known as Fraser Island, 190 kilometres north of Brisbane, was World Heritage listed in 1992 along with the Cooloola sand mass. Fraser is the world's largest sand island and a unique wilderness area, with towering white sand dunes, freshwater lakes containing remarkable waterlife and rainforests of surpassing beauty. Conservationists early realised the value of Fraser, and today the many visitors who enjoy its wonders are conscious of the fragility of its habitats and take due care to preserve them.

Fraser Island lakes

A crystal clear Lake McKenzie reflects the azure sky.

Opposite: Lake Jennings.

Fraser Island's freshwater lakes are renowned worldwide. They range in colour from palest blue-green to golden-brown and teem with wildlife. From July to September each year, the heathlands which surround many of these lakes are brilliant with wildflowers and alive with birds.

Unique forests

The forests of Fraser Island, rooted in pure sand and sustained by a remarkable cycle of growth, decay and rebirth, were the object of a long struggle between timber interests and conservationists. The island is now listed as a World Heritage site, and it is to be hoped that the splendid brush boxes, kauri pines and satinays of its rainforests will continue to delight future generations. To wander these forests, discovering crystal creeks running over beds of pure white sand, is to enter another world.

The northern half of Fraser Island is included in the Great Sandy National Park: the sand dune systems of this region are the largest and oldest in the world, and were first formed more than 30 000 years ago.

Left: Wanggoolba Creek winds through rainforest on Fraser Island.

Sandy Cape

The lighthouse at Sandy Cape, on the northern tip of Fraser Island..

A Portuguese navigator, de Menonca, may have visited Fraser Island around 1521. Captain Cook, its official European discoverer, sailed past in 1770. The island was named after Captain and Eliza Fraser, who reached it in 1836 after shipwreck. Although Captain Fraser did not survive encounters with the Aborigines, Mrs Fraser did, and her experiences have become the basis for several books and a film.

A perched lake, awesome sand dunes and unspoiled beach – the quintessential Fraser Island scene.

The number of vessels wrecked in the waters around Fraser Island was of such concern that a lighthouse 20 metres in height was erected at Sandy Cape, on the northern tip of the island, in 1870. However, wrecks continued to occur. Best-known are the *Marloo*, an Italian luxury yacht which beached in 1914 north of Waddy Point, and the *Maheno*, a former World War I hospital ship which grounded during a cyclone in 1935.

The dramatic cliffs of Indian Head, Fraser Island.

Hervey Bay, where a two-week Whale Festival is held each August.

Whale-watching craft operate under strict rules so they do not alarm the whales.

Male Humpback Whales showing off, perhaps to a female.

Individual whales can be identified by the patterns on their tail flukes.

Hervey Bay

In springtime, Humpback Whales make the long migration from their feeding grounds in Antarctic waters to their breeding grounds in the warm waters of northern Australia. Females give birth and suckle their young, males compete for the attention of unmated females and the sounds of whale-song echo through the blue Pacific.

Hervey Bay is a place where whales can rest and relax on their epic journey, and the whale-watchers who gather there from August to October each year take precautions not to alarm the ocean giants. Many whales seem to accept the presence of cruise vessels; observers are particularly excited when the leviathans breach, rising from the water then falling back with a thunderous crash. Sometimes a whale approaches so close to craft that the sound of its breathy exhalation mingles with the rapid clicking of cameras and the awed gasps of the appreciative observers.

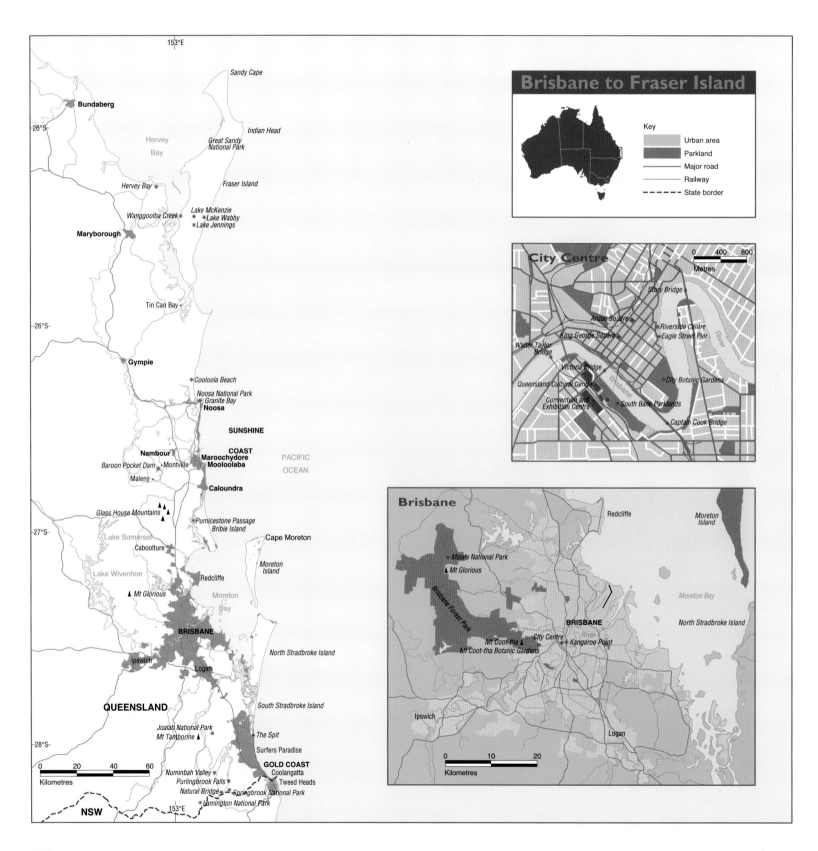

Brisbane to Fraser Island

Key
Urban area
Parkland
Major road
Railway
State border

City Centre

Story Bridge
Anzac Square
Riverside Centre
King George Square
Eagle Street Pier
Walter Taylor Bridge
Victoria Bridge
City Botanic Gardens
Queensland Cultural Centre
Convention and Exhibition Centre
South Bank Parklands
Captain Cook Bridge
Brisbane River

0   400   800
Metres

Brisbane

Redcliffe
Moreton Island
Maiala National Park
Mt Glorious
Brisbane Forest Park
Moreton Bay
BRISBANE
Mt Coot-tha
City Centre
Kangaroo Point
North Stradbroke Island
Mt Coot-tha Botanic Gardens
Brisbane River
Ipswich
Logan

0   10   20
Kilometres

153°E
Sandy Cape
Bundaberg
26°S
Hervey Bay
Indian Head
Great Sandy National Park
Hervey Bay
Fraser Island
Wanggoolba Creek
Lake McKenzie
Lake Wabby
Lake Jennings
Maryborough
26°S
Tin Can Bay
Gympie
Cooloola Beach
Noosa National Park
Granite Bay
Noosa
SUNSHINE
COAST
Nambour
Maroochydore
Baroon Pocket Dam
Montville
Mooloolaba
Maleny
Caloundra
PACIFIC
OCEAN
Glass House Mountains
27°S
Pumicestone Passage
Bribie Island
Lake Somerset
Cape Moreton
Caboolture
Moreton Island
Lake Wivenhoe
Redcliffe
Mt Glorious
Moreton Bay
BRISBANE
North Stradbroke Island
Ipswich
Logan
QUEENSLAND
South Stradbroke Island
Joalah National Park
Mt Tamborine
The Spit
28°S
Surfers Paradise
GOLD COAST
Coolangatta
Numinbah Valley
Purlingbrook Falls
Tweed Heads
Natural Bridge
Springbrook National Park
Lamington National Park
NSW
153°E

0   20   40   60
Kilometres

Exploring Great Sandy National Park.

Discovering Brisbane and beyond

As a base for anyone with the urge to adventure, to explore and to record the country's beauty on film, Brisbane is unequalled. The city itself offers wonderful visual challenges, with its expanses of river, its mixture of glittering high-rises and ornate colonial buildings, and its lush green spaces. The coastline to the north and south of Brisbane, and the remarkable rainforests and eucalypt parklands of the ranges to its west, are a photographer's delight.

A four-wheel-drive is handy for mountainous and coastal exploration, but the traveller should remember that rainforest, coastal heathland and shorelines are particularly fragile ecosystems which should be treated with care. The wheel tracks shown on pages 100-101 may wash away with the tide, but the creatures which live just beneath the sand's surface feel their impact.

Nature has showered gifts upon south-east Queensland. It is one of the world's greatest playgrounds and its natural beauty should be treasured and respected.

Steve Parish

World-famous photographer Steve Parish began his remarkable career by recording marine life off Australia's coasts. After discovering the fascinations of the rainforest and its wild creatures, he has spent much of his life journeying around Australia photographing the landscapes, plants, animals and the people of the land. Of recent years, he has extended the range of his subjects to include Australia's cities and towns.

The magnificent library of images which has resulted has become the heart of Steve Parish Publishing Pty Ltd. Through the firm's publications, Steve and his wife and partner Jan are realising their dream of sharing Australia with the world.

Celebrating Australia is a collection of titles which present the incomparable beauty of the southern continent in superb photographs and text. As Steve comments: "After a lifetime of travel and asking questions, I have only just begun to discover how much there is to learn about Australia. I hope these books arouse in others a desire like mine to explore and to appreciate this wonderful country."

Index

First published by Steve Parish Publishing Pty Ltd, 1997
PO Box 2160, Fortitude Valley BC, Queensland 4006, Australia
© copyright Steve Parish Publishing Pty Ltd, 1997
ISBN 1 875932 99 2
Photography: Steve Parish
Text: Pat Slater, Steve Parish Publishing, Australia

Map supplied by MAPgraphics
Editing, design: Steve Parish Publishing, Australia
Printed in Hong Kong
Colour separations by Steve Parish Publishing, Australia